ANGER
Facing the Fire Within

JUNE HUNT

ROSE PUBLISHING/ASPIRE PRESS

Carson, California

ROSE PUBLISHING/ASPIRE PRESS

Anger: Facing the Fire Within
Copyright © 2013 Hope For The Heart
All rights reserved.
Aspire Press, a division of Rose Publishing, Inc.
17909 Adria Maru Lane
Carson, California 90746 USA
www.aspirepress.com

Register your book at www.aspirepress.com/register
Get inspiration via email, sign up at www.aspirepress.com

The information and solutions offered in this resource are
a result of years of Bible study, research, and practical life
application. They are intended as guidelines for healthy living
and are not a replacement for professional medical advice
and counseling. JUNE HUNT and HOPE FOR THE HEART
make no warranties, representations, or guarantees regarding
any particular result or outcome. Any and all express or
implied warranties are disclaimed. Please consult qualified
medical, pastoral, and psychological professionals regarding
individual conditions and needs. JUNE HUNT and HOPE
FOR THE HEART do not advocate that you treat yourself or
someone you know and disclaim any and all liability arising
directly or indirectly from the information in this resource.

For more information on Hope For The Heart, visit
www.hopefortheheart.org or call 1-800-488-HOPE (4673).

Printed by Regent Publishing Services Ltd.
Printed in China
March 2017, 11th printing

CONTENTS

ear friend,

When people see me, they don't see me as an "angry person." And most of the time, I'm not. Yet, how well I remember *that* day—the scenario remains vivid in my mind: I opened my friend's desk drawer (something I had never done before) to get a few paper clips. Within a few seconds, I was staring at a piece of paper with these words, *"We don't need any more June Hunts in this world."* I was stunned—I was hurt—I was frustrated … I was angry! Just an hour before, the writer of those words had said to me, *"I'm really for you. I want to help you. I want to support you."* (Some support!) How deeply the words had cut my heart!

Immediately, I felt intense anger welling up inside me. I knew that if I didn't find a way to reduce the pressure, I would explode onto my "friend." So I thought to myself, *I need to go outside and jog— that will release my pent-up energy.*

Having laced up my tennis shoes, I walked out the front door ready to defeat my anger through my walking/jogging/walking routine. A few moments into my trek, I noticed my arms swinging higher than normal. I even said to myself, *This is really unusual!*

After 20 minutes, I wasn't feeling any relief. I had expected the jogging to be like releasing a valve on a pressure cooker, but it wasn't working— the valve over my heart was stuck! In fact, the

longer I jogged, the deeper my hurt went. I soon realized why—I had been rehearsing, over and over, how much I had been wronged … deceived … betrayed.

Of course, the Bible says, *"[Love] keeps no record of wrongs"* (1 Corinthians 13:5). This I knew. I certainly was not helping myself.

I remember thinking, *I'm not feeling any better—I have to do something else.* Then I started praying, *"Lord, teach me to act rather than react."* Actually, I said those words over and over: *"Lord, teach me to act rather than react. Teach me to act rather than react. …"* Soon I noticed that I was praying those words to the rhythmic pattern of my running as my tennis shoes hit the pavement.

At the end of an hour, my heart was at peace. I was no longer being controlled by that debilitating sense of betrayal. Of course, the initial problem wasn't solved—confrontation would still be necessary. But I was able to release my anger to the Lord that night, as well as the situation that caused it. Then the next day during the confrontation, my anger did return, but this time I was able to control it rather than let it control me.

Ever since that day, when I feel a strong sense of anger, *if*—that is *if*—I remember to pray sincerely, *"Lord, teach me to act rather than react,"* God gives me His grace and power to weigh my words and speak with self-control.

Today as you look at anger in your own life and look for the *answer to anger*, I pray that you too will say, *"Lord, teach me to act rather than react,"* and then lean on Him for the strength to do it.

Yours in the Lord's hope,

June

June Hunt

P.S. From my simple prayer, born out of anger, came a song. And contained within this song, toward the end, are these words:

When I feel disappointment with no soothing
ointment, and nothing is going my way,
When my heart has been breaking and my soul is
aching, and I have no more words to say.

I'm not under illusion, the only solution
is die to my rights each day,
Because Christ is inside me to comfort and guide
me, and His life has taught me to pray.

Lord, teach me to act rather than react,
with Your Spirit in control of me.
Lord, teach me to help rather than hinder,
with the Lord being Lord of me.

Lord, teach me to trust rather than mistrust,
with Your Spirit inside my soul.
Lord, teach me to act rather than react,
I give You complete control.

ANGER
Facing the Fire Within

The day begins like any other day, but ends like no other, for on this day, he gives full vent to his anger and, as a result, finds himself running for his life.

He is part of a mistreated minority—grievously persecuted—not for doing something wrong, but for being perceived as a threat. Raised with privilege in the palace of a "king," he had been spared the heartless treatment inflicted on his kinsmen. But watching the injustice day after day and year after year finally becomes too much for him to bear.

When he sees one of his own people suffering an inhumane beating at the hands of an Egyptian, Moses is filled with rage. He snaps. In an instant, he kills the Egyptian and hides the body in the sand. But his angry, impetuous act is not committed in secret. When news of the murder reaches Pharaoh, Moses fears for his life and flees. (See Exodus chapter 2.)

When you look at the life of Moses, you can see both the power and the problems inherent in anger. Has anger ever clouded your judgment to the point that you reacted rashly ... and lived to regret it? Ultimately, you have the choice to *act* wisely or to *react* foolishly. In his lifetime, Moses *did both*. Like him, you too can face the fiery anger within and *learn to keep it under control*. In doing so, you will demonstrate wisdom because ...

> "A fool gives full vent to his anger, but
> a wise man keeps himself under control."
> (Proverbs 29:11)

DEFINITIONS

INJUSTICE IGNITES ANGER

Understandably, Moses felt anger over the *unjust* treatment of his Hebrew brothers, but what he did with that anger is what caused all the trouble. Moses allowed his anger to overpower him. Acting on impulse, he committed a crime—he committed murder.

Although he was right about the *injustice*, he was wrong in his reaction. His hot-blooded volatility revealed how unprepared he was for the task God had planned for him. Consequently, God kept Moses on the back side of a desert for the next 40 years so that he would realize that rescuing his own people *in his own way* would ultimately fail.

Moses needed to learn this vital lesson well to become the leader through whom God would accomplish His own will *in His own supernatural way*. In truth, Moses had tried to earn the Israelites' respect by coming to their rescue. Instead, his murderous rage earned only their disrespect.

"Moses thought that his own people would realize that God was using him to rescue them, but they did not."
(Acts 7:25)

What had begun as a smoldering ember in the heart of Moses quickly burst into deadly flames. Perhaps no one noticed the angry sparks flying from his eyes, but his spirit was consumed with the heat of anger.

> "Glancing this way and that and seeing no one, he killed the Egyptian and hid him in the sand." (Exodus 2:12)

Who hasn't lit a candle and become entranced by the flickering flame? As it dances on the wick, it is a delight to see, but dangerous to touch. No one dares put a finger into even the tiniest of blazes.

Anger is much like the flame of a candle—it's associated with "heat" of varying degrees. Temperatures are determined by the hues of the flame, but no matter the blues, yellows, oranges, and reds, we all know that *it's hot*, and if we hold on to it, we will get burned!

And so it is with anger: The higher the degree of heat, the more people get hurt—*including you.*

> "Can a man scoop fire into his lap without his clothes being burned?" (Proverbs 6:27)

▶ **Anger** is a strong emotion of irritation or agitation that occurs when a need or expectation is not met.[1]

"An angry man stirs up dissension, and a hot-tempered one commits many sins." (Proverbs 29:22)

▶ **Angry** people in the Bible are often described as *hot-tempered* and *quick-tempered.*

"A hot-tempered man stirs up dissension, but a patient man calms a quarrel." (Proverbs 15:18)

▶ **Anger** in the Old Testament is most frequently the Hebrew word *aph*, literally meaning "nose or nostrils," figuratively depicting nostrils flaring with anger. Later, *aph* came to represent the entire face as seen in two ancient Hebrew idioms:[2]

- "Long of face" (or nose), meaning *slow to anger.*

  "The LORD is gracious and compassionate, slow to anger and rich in love." (Psalm 145:8)

- "Short of face" (or nose), meaning *quick to anger.*

  "A quick-tempered man does foolish things." (Proverbs 14:17)

In the New Testament, the Greek word *orge* originally meant any "natural impulse or desire," but later came to signify "anger as the strongest of all passions." It is often translated as "wrath" because of its powerful, lasting nature.[3]

"For those who are self-seeking and who reject the truth and follow evil, there will be wrath and anger." (Romans 2:8)

WHAT IS the Magnitude of Anger?

The next time you light a candle, allow your eyes to scan the scintillating hues and shades of the flame. Notice the light blue at the center—that's actually the hottest part of the flame, measuring 1,400° Celsius (2,552° F). The temperature then diminishes from the inner core to the outer sides, signified by shades of yellow, orange, then red, at 800° Celsius (1,472° F).

Likewise, anger can run the gamut from bright red to a light blue. Anger can lightly singe, or severely scorch. It ranges from mild agitation to hot explosions, from

controlled irritations to uncontrolled eruptions. In the Bible, Joseph's two brothers displayed the destructive heat of anger.

> "Simeon and Levi ... have killed men in their anger ... Cursed be their anger, so fierce, and their fury, so cruel!" (Genesis 49:5–7)

Anger is a wide umbrella word covering many levels of the emotion.[4]

▶ **Indignation is simmering anger** provoked by something appearing to be unjust or unkind and often perceived as justified. Jesus became "indignant" when the disciples prevented parents from bringing their children to Him so that He might touch and bless them.

> *"When Jesus saw this, he was indignant. He said to them, 'Let the little children come to me, and do not hinder them, for the kingdom of God belongs to such as these.'"* (Mark 10:14)

▶ **Wrath is burning anger** accompanied by a desire to avenge. Wrath often moves from the inner emotion of anger to the outer expression of anger. In Romans 1:18 God expresses His wrath as divine judgment on those who commit willful sin.

> *"The wrath of God is being revealed from heaven against all the godlessness and wickedness of men who suppress the truth by their wickedness."* (Romans 1:18)

▶ **Fury is fiery anger** so fierce that it destroys common sense. The word *fury* suggests a powerful force compelled to harm or destroy. Some members of the Sanhedrin were so angry with Peter and the other apostles for proclaiming

Jesus was God that *"they were furious and wanted to put them to death"* (Acts 5:33). This is why the Bible says, *"Anger is cruel and fury overwhelming"* (Proverbs 27:4).

▶ **Rage is blazing anger** resulting in loss of self-control, often to the extreme of violence and temporary insanity. After an outburst of rage, a cry of remorseful regret or disbelief is often expressed—"I can't believe I did that!" Yet those who continue to vent their rage toward others, including toward God, find themselves defeated by their own destructive decisions and ruined relationships.

"A man's own folly ruins his life, yet his heart rages against the LORD." (Proverbs 19:3)

WHAT IS the Misuse of Anger?

Periodically, everyone feels the heat of anger, but how you handle the heat determines whether or not you are misusing it. The small flame that lights a cozy campfire, if left unchecked, can just as quickly ignite a fierce forest fire. Conversely, the initial spark of anger that could be used for good, if snuffed out too quickly, can keep anger from accomplishing its designated purpose. If you are wise, you have learned how to handle your anger, and you have learned how to help others handle their anger.[5] The Bible says ...

> **"Wise men turn away anger."**
> **(Proverbs 29:8)**

▶ **Prolonged anger**—the *"simmering stew"*—is held in for a long time. This anger is a result of an unforgiving heart toward a past offense and the

offender. Unforgiveness left unresolved eventually results in resentment and bitterness, ultimately scalding close relationships

EXAMPLE: "I'll never forgive the way he talked to me years ago."

But the Bible says, *"See to it that no one misses the grace of God and that no bitter root grows up to cause trouble and defile many."* (Hebrews 12:15)

▶ **Pressed-down anger**—the *"pressure cooker"*—is denied or hidden anger. Usually developing from a fear of facing negative emotions, this kind of anger can create a deceitful heart and lead to untruthfulness with others. Failure to honestly confront and resolve angry feelings can result in self-pity, self-contempt, and self-doubt, ultimately searing close relationships.

EXAMPLE: "I never get angry—maybe just a little irritated at times."

But the Bible says, *"Whoever would love life and see good days must keep his tongue from evil and his lips from deceitful speech."* (1 Peter 3:10)

▶ **Provoked anger**—the *"short fuse"*—is quick and impatient, instantly irritated or incensed. A testy temper is often expressed using criticism or sarcasm under the guise of teasing, ultimately burning close relationships.

EXAMPLE: "I can't believe you said that! You're so childish!"

But the Bible says, *"Do not be quickly provoked in your spirit, for anger resides in the lap of fools."* (Ecclesiastes 7:9)

▶ **Profuse anger**—the *"volatile volcano"*—is powerful, destructive, hard to control. This way of releasing anger is characterized by contempt, violence, and abuse toward others, ultimately cremating close relationships.

EXAMPLE: "You fool—if you do that again, you'll wish you'd never been born!"

But Jesus says, *"I tell you that anyone who is angry with his brother will be subject to judgment. ... But anyone who says, 'You fool!' will be in danger of the fire of hell."* (Matthew 5:22)

Misplaced Anger

QUESTION: **"Why do some people take their anger out on an innocent bystander—those who have nothing to do with the problem?"**

ANSWER: Imagine, after having a flat tire, the boss begins yelling at his employee ... who in turn arrives home and yells at his wife ... who then screams at their son ... who in turn kicks the cat! This could be called "The Blame Game."

Ultimately, angry people who are afraid to confront those who hurt them will often pick targets they can safely overpower. Their easy "victory" inflates their sense of power, giving them a false sense of significance.

▶ **Bullies** are known for misplacing their anger onto weaker, more vulnerable people. More often than not, bullying is a case of "playing it safe" and venting on someone who can't fight back. The bully's stored up anger generally comes from being abused by someone they feel powerless to confront.

► **Abusers** commonly spew out their anger on those closest to them—those most vulnerable to them. Almost all abusive adults were abused as children and grew up with the intense pressure of unresolved anger. When their anger ignites, for whatever reason, everyone around them feels the explosion and falls victim to their blistering, lava-like anger.

► **Self-injurious** people generally carry a sizable amount of self-contempt and self-loathing. As children, many were falsely blamed for family problems and assigned the role of family scapegoat. They internalized the lies spoken to them, and now as adults they are quick to assume blame for all that goes wrong around them. The anger they could rightly feel toward others, they wrongly aim back at themselves—anger they are quick to receive.

► **Self-protectors** haven't the strength of character to express their anger toward the people causing their anger. (They are the ones who kick the cat when they would really like to kick the boss!) They express anger in detrimental, subversive ways.

Unfortunately, a prevalent cause of home fires is flaming candles left unattended on furniture. The scene is sadly common. The candle melts and spreads across a flammable surface that catches fire, which quickly engulfs the room. Lighted candles convey a certain charm, putting off a warm glow, often releasing a pleasantly fragrant aroma, pleasing and delighting all present. But when the flame travels from candle to furniture, it's frightening. So it is with misplaced anger that engulfs an innocent person. Rather than being positive, it produces only pain. In the case of King Saul, his misplaced anger toward David resulted in the murder of 85 priests of God.

"Saul said to him,
'Why have you conspired against me,
you and the son of Jesse,
giving him bread and a sword
and inquiring of God for him,
so that he has rebelled against me
and lies in wait for me, as he does today?'
Ahimelech answered the king ...
'Let not the king accuse your servant
or any of his father's family,
for your servant knows nothing at all
about this whole affair.' ...
The king then ordered Doeg,
'You turn and strike down the priests.'
So Doeg the Edomite turned and struck them
down. That day he killed eighty-five men
who wore the linen ephod."
(1 Samuel 22:13–15, 18)

WHAT ARE Misconceptions about Anger?

Every day, people leave their homes—perhaps just *for a moment*—only to return to experience the loss *of a lifetime*. Misconceptions about the fiery potential of even a small votive candle can result in utter ruin.

A candle, in and of itself, is not dangerous, but miscalculations about candles can be extremely dangerous. Placing a candle next to a can of oil can be catastrophic.

Misconceptions about anger can also create a dangerous environment, resulting in devastating emotions.

Do you always view anger as negative and sinful? Do you seek to hide your anger from others, even from

yourself in hopes of snuffing it out? Misunderstandings about anger give this powerful emotion a less than positive reputation! If you are blind to God's purposes for anger and if you are afraid of revealing your true feelings, you may be in bondage to ignorance or false guilt. The Bible says ...

"Surely you desire truth in the inner parts;
you teach me wisdom in the inmost place."
(Psalm 51:6)

Anger and Sin

QUESTION: "Is it a sin for me to be angry?"

ANSWER: No. The initial feeling of anger is a God-given emotion. The way you express your anger determines whether or not it becomes sin. The Bible says ...

"In your anger do not sin."
(Psalm 4:4)

Anger and Guilt

QUESTION: "How can I keep from feeling guilty when I'm angry?"[6]

ANSWER: Your anger is a signal—like the red warning light on the dashboard of a car—indicating: *Something's wrong, something's wrong, something's wrong!* And the purpose of the light is *to propel you to action,* to cause you to stop, evaluate what is wrong, then take appropriate action. Jesus became angry at the hypocritical religious leaders who took an extreme position regarding "resting on the Sabbath"—even teaching that healing the sick on the Sabbath was an offense worthy of the death penalty. In sharp contrast,

Jesus intentionally and fully restored a man's crippled hand on the Sabbath.

"He looked around at them in anger and, deeply distressed at their stubborn hearts, said to the man, 'Stretch out your hand.' He stretched it out, and his hand was completely restored."
(Mark 3:5)

Anger and God's Nature

QUESTION: "How can a God of love be a God of wrath at the same time?"[7]

ANSWER: Since some people don't understand how a loving God can possess the attribute of "wrath," let's look at those two characteristics on a personal level. Because of God's great love for you, He directs His anger toward anyone or anything that thwarts His perfect plan for you. God's anger never operates independently of His love, but rather He expresses anger on your behalf and for your ultimate good.

"This is what the Lord Almighty says ... 'whoever touches you touches the apple of his eye.'"
(Zechariah 2:8)

Anger—People Not Appearing Angry

QUESTION: "Can people be angry even when they don't look or sound angry?"

ANSWER: Yes. Many people have difficulty expressing or even recognizing their emotion of anger. Instead, they have learned to deny, ignore, or repress their anger by burying it deep within their hearts. However, our anger is not hidden from God, who sees it and understands it.

"Nothing in all creation is hidden from God's sight. Everything is uncovered and laid bare before the eyes of him to whom we must give account. ... The LORD searches every heart and understands every motive behind the thoughts."
(Hebrews 4:13; 1 Chronicles 28:9)

CHARACTERISTICS OF ANGER

HURT IGNITES ANGER

Betrayal by an enemy certainly hurts our feelings, but betrayal by a friend deeply wounds the soul. Everyone expects opposition from those on the outside, but what do you do when opposition comes from within—from among your own circle, your closest confidants, your trusted few?

One national leader knew the *hurt* of such betrayal. He had led wisely, demonstrated courage, and won the confidence of his people. *He was there for them*— and they knew it.

However, his authority was undermined by a subordinate who created such dissension that he successfully stole the loyalty of 250 others. Those the leader had trusted throughout the years, those who knew him best, those who should have been most loyal, turned against him. In response, however, Moses did not express his anger by taking personal revenge—he did not react impulsively—but rather appealed to the Lord to act on his behalf. *"Moses became very angry and said to the* Lord, *'Do not accept their offering. I have not ... wronged any of them.'"* (Numbers 16:15)

Although justifiably angry, Moses had learned how to face the fiery anger within and to *act wisely rather than to react foolishly*. He restrained his rage, poured out his heart, and pleaded with the Lord to deal with his offenders. In turn, God took up his cause, destroyed his betrayers, and defended his honor. Moses refused

to take revenge, but rather allowed the Lord to be his avenger because God had given this promise: *"It is mine to avenge; I will repay."* (Deuteronomy 32:35)

WHAT ARE Your "Anger Cues"?

When it comes to "picturing" anger, perhaps the most poignant illustration would be one of those cragged, gargantuan land formations that sputter with steam and spew molten rock—*the volcano.*

Like anger, before a toxic flow emerges, there is a gurgling beneath the surface, a swirling series of events that creates instability and sets the stage for an explosive outburst. Scientists have learned how to look for "cues" that a volcano is about to erupt, including the release of steam and gases, small earthquakes and tremors, and swelling of the volcano's slopes.

Similarly, the human body has a *physical reaction* when it experiences anger. These anger cues can alert you when you begin to feel angry. Discerning your own anger cues can help you avoid trouble. Likewise, being aware of the signs of anger in others can alert you to defend yourself, just like a firefighter defends himself by wearing fire-retardant clothing.

A biblical example of an anger cue is Jonathan's loss of appetite when he was hurt and grieved over his father's unjust, shameful treatment toward his close friend David. *"Jonathan got up from the table in fierce anger ... he did not eat, because he was grieved at his father's shameful treatment of David."* (1 Samuel 20:34)

Anger Cues Checklist

In seeking to identify your anger cues, place a check mark (✓) beside the following questions that are true of you:

☐ Do you have a decreased appetite?

☐ Do you have tense muscles?

☐ Do you feel unusually hot or cold?

☐ Do you have increased perspiration?

☐ Do you feel flushed?

☐ Do you clench your teeth?

☐ Do you clench your fists?

☐ Do you experience dry mouth?

☐ Do you become silent—shutting down verbally?

☐ Do you use loud, rapid, or high-pitched speech?

☐ Do you breathe faster and harder than normal?

☐ Do you experience an upset, churning stomach?

☐ Do you walk hard and fast or pace back and forth?

☐ Do you have twitches or anxious behaviors (such as tapping a pencil, shaking a foot)?

☐ Do you use language that is inappropriate, harsh, or coarse, including gossip and sarcasm?

☐ Do you feel your heart racing?

Once you have identified your anger cues, you will be in a better position to quickly identify when you are angry. Then you can direct your energies to produce a positive outcome. (See 2 Corinthians 7:10–11)

A volcanic crater contains toxic gases, a steaming underbelly, and razor-sharp rock fragments. Deep within the heart of unresolved anger, the darkened deposits of a critical spirit—*bitterness and depression* (among others)—can be found.

When volcanologists excavate and analyze material inside a crater, they work as quickly and efficiently as possible, being aware that the longer they stay, the higher the risk of injury or even death.[8] And so it is with *unresolved* anger. The longer it's allowed to fume and fester, the more dangerous—and even deadly—it can be for you and those around you.

Prolonged anger fans the flame of bitterness and fuels unforgiveness. Refusing to face your feelings in a healthy way prolongs *unresolved* anger until it eventually becomes *harbored* anger.

Unresolved anger not only creates a rift between you and God, but also damages your body, destroys your emotions, and demoralizes your relationships. Whether you recognize it or not, extended anger can cause significant physical, emotional, and spiritual problems. Jesus said ...

> "I tell you that anyone who is angry with his brother will be subject to judgment."
> (Matthew 5:22)

Unresolved anger is known to produce in many people some of the following physical, emotional, and spiritual symptoms:[9]

▶ **Physical Symptoms**

- Blurred vision
- Headaches
- Heart disease
- High blood pressure
- Insomnia
- Intestinal disorders
- Overeating
- Stomach disorders

▶ **Emotional Symptoms**

- Anxiety
- Bitterness
- Compulsions
- Depression
- Fear
- Insecurity
- Phobias
- Worry

▶ **Spiritual Symptoms**

- Loss of confidence: Feeling insecure about your relationship with God and your ability to respond wisely to difficulties
- Loss of energy: Lacking strength for your service to God and others
- Loss of faith: Failing to believe that God is working in your life
- Loss of freedom: Becoming a prisoner of your emotions and unable to serve God freely
- Loss of identity: Becoming like the person toward whom you are bitter rather than becoming like Christ
- Loss of perspective: Allowing your emotions to distort your thinking
- Loss of sensitivity: Failing to hear the Spirit of God speaking to your heart
- Loss of vision: Losing a sense of God's purpose for your life

Most volcanic craters are about as deep as a football field is wide—*100 yards*. They are dark, mysterious places with deposits tracing eruptions from hundreds, even thousands, of years before. One of the most well-known volcanoes in recent history has been Mount St. Helens in Washington State. The rumbling and raging mountain sent a pyrotechnic blast of ash and molten rock over more than 230 square miles and, in May of 1980, killed 57 people.[10]

Other eruptions of Mount St. Helens have since occurred, but not with such catastrophic results. Actually, they have served to clue scientists in to an interesting fact: The magma driving the most recent volcanic activity was likely left over from the 1980s eruption.

In similar ways, the hidden anger from childhood hurts can *directly* affect present-day outbursts. Many people live life unaware that they have hidden anger—suppressed anger that only occasionally surfaces. While this hidden anger is usually rooted in past childhood hurts, the underlying effects are always ready to surface and can sizzle up an already simmering scenario. For example, when someone says or does something "wrong," the one with suppressed anger often overreacts. When someone makes an innocent mistake, the magnitude of anger is out of proportion to the mistake.

If you have hidden anger, you can find yourself at one extreme or another—from feeling hopeless to feeling hostile—and yet be totally unaware of why you are experiencing these feelings. The Bible makes it clear that some of our motives and emotions are hidden

from our own view. *"Who can discern his errors? Forgive my hidden faults."* (Psalm 19:12)

Anger and Irrational Thinking

QUESTION: **"Why do some angry people become irrational in their thinking?"**[11]

ANSWER: When people are angry, their problem-solving ability plummets because ...

▶ Inside the body, epinephrine (adrenaline) is released by the adrenal glands, immediately preparing the body for "fight or flight." However, if "fight or flight" does not occur, the highly energized body has difficulty calming down. (This is why angry people experience racing heart, shaking hands, and fast breathing.)

▶ The angry person's hormones then travel from the brain to the adrenal glands, signaling the need for tension reduction by the release of cortisol. However, cortisol raises blood pressure above the norm, which makes rational thinking more difficult.

King Saul provides an example of irrational thinking in his anger toward his son Jonathan.

"Saul's anger flared up at Jonathan and he said to him, 'You son of a perverse and rebellious woman! Don't I know that you have sided with the son of Jesse to your own shame and to the shame of the mother who bore you? As long as the son of Jesse lives on this earth, neither you nor your kingdom will be established. Now send and bring him to me, for he must die!'" (1 Samuel 20:30–31)

Clues to Find Hidden Anger Checklist

Place a check mark (✓) beside the questions that are true of you:

☐ Do you become irritable over trifles?

☐ Do you smile on the outside while you hurt or rage on the inside?

☐ Do you find your identity and worth in excessive work?

☐ Do you deny ever being impatient?

☐ Do you have to have the last word?

☐ Do those close to you say that you blame others?

☐ Do you feel emotionally flat?

☐ Do you find yourself quickly fatigued?

☐ Do you have a loss of interest in life?

☐ Do you become easily frustrated?

If you find you have hidden anger, follow this clear directive from the Word of God.

> "You must rid yourselves of all such things as these: anger, rage, malice, slander, and filthy language from your lips."
> (Colossians 3:8)

DO YOU *Act* or *React* When You Are Angry?[12]

Scientists are continually developing technology to help them "act" in preparation for a volcanic eruption, rather than simply "react" to its deadly blast and lava after the fact.

In recent years monitoring devices known as "spiders" (because of their spindly legs) have been used to crawl around the interior of craters and measure seismic activity. The creator of the device, Rick LaHusen, a hydrologist at the Cascades Volcano Observatory in Vancouver, Canada, observed: "They can analyze their data in real time and decide what's important and what's not important and prioritize it."[13]

People who choose to act rather than react to anger share some similarities with the analytical "spiders"— reason rules the day, and predetermined preparedness can help avert great tragedy.

When you are angry, does reason rule the day or do tense emotions take over? Do you allow the mind of Christ within you to make choices that lead to *appropriate actions,* or do you have knee-jerk reactions that lead to *inappropriate reactions*? If you have never evaluated what happens when you feel angry, or if you don't know how others perceive you when you are angry, seek God's wisdom and understanding.

> "If you call out for insight and
> cry aloud for understanding,
> and if you look for it as for silver
> and search for it as for hidden treasure,
> then you will understand the fear of the LORD
> and find the knowledge of God.
> For the LORD gives wisdom, and from his mouth

come knowledge and understanding."
(Proverbs 2:3–6)

Appropriate actions express your thoughts and feelings with restraint, understanding, and concern for the other person's welfare.

"A man of knowledge uses words with restraint,
and a man of understanding is even-tempered."
(Proverbs 17:27)

Inappropriate reactions express your thoughts and feelings in such a way that stirs up anger in others and produces strife. The biblical Book of Wisdom, paints this graphic picture.

"As churning the milk produces butter,
and as twisting the nose produces blood,
so stirring up anger produces strife."
(Proverbs 30:33)

Act or React Checklist

To help assess whether you act in or react to anger, take time to answer the following questions and place a check mark (✓) beside those that are true of you:

Appropriate Actions

☐ Do you use tactful, compassionate words?

☐ Do you see the other person's point of view?

☐ Do you want to help the one who angers you?

☐ Do you focus on your own faults?

☐ Do you have realistic expectations?

☐ Do you have a flexible and cooperative attitude?

☐ Do you forgive personal injustices?

☐ Do you act in a gracious way, trusting God with the outcome?

☐ Do you trust God to exercise justice according to His timing?

Inappropriate Reactions

☐ Do you use tactless, condemning words?

☐ Do you see only your point of view?

☐ Do you want to punish the one who angers you?

☐ Do you focus only on the faults of others?

☐ Do you have unrealistic expectations?

☐ Do you have a rigid and uncooperative attitude?

☐ Do you have difficulty forgiving injustices?

☐ Do you manipulate or intimidate to control the outcome?

☐ Do you insist on justice according to your timing?

Even though a situation may evoke anger, those who allow the Lord to be their strength will respond appropriately. (See Colossians 3:12.)

CAUSES OF ANGER

FEAR IGNITES ANGER

Imagine leading thousands of people through the desert with all of them looking to you to meet both their physical and spiritual needs. While setting up camp at the base of a mountain, God calls you to climb the mountain and meet with Him because He plans to give you the Ten Commandments and other beneficial laws.

As you meet with God, unbeknownst to you, the very people God has instructed you to lead have turned their hearts away from Him. They melt their precious gold, mold a golden calf, and merrily worship it! Now, God interrupts your meeting to inform you that your people have turned against Him. Flushed with anger and fear, you rush down the mountain to confront them.

Exodus 32:19 states, *"When Moses approached the camp and saw the calf and the dancing, his anger burned and he threw the tablets out of his hands, breaking them to pieces at the foot of the mountain."*

Moses reacted in anger because he was full of fear. He was afraid God's righteous anger against his disobedient people would result in their destruction. (That very day 3,000 disobedient Israelites died and the people were struck with a plague.) He knew they needed to *"Worship God acceptably with reverence and awe, for our 'God is a consuming fire.'"* (Hebrews 12:28–29)

Throughout the natural world, unexpected fires can be started and fueled by at least four sources: seeping oil, seeping gas, molten lava, or coal bed methane (a flammable gas that can cause mining explosions). In a similar way, anger is typically started and fueled by at least 1 of 4 sources: hurt, injustice, fear, or frustration. Therefore, anger is a secondary response to 1 or more of these 4 roots.

Probing into buried feelings from your past can be painful. Therefore, it can seem easier to stay angry than to uncover the cause, turn loose of your "rights," and grow in maturity.[14] When you are seeking to uproot problematic anger, you must have perseverance because ...

> "Perseverance must finish its work so that you may be mature and complete, not lacking anything." (James 1:4)

1 HURT: Your heart is wounded.[15]

Everyone has a God-given inner need for *unconditional love*.[16] When you experience rejection or emotional pain of any kind, anger can become a protective wall keeping people, pain, and *hurt* away.

BIBLICAL EXAMPLE: The Sons of Jacob
Joseph was the undisputed favorite among Jacob's sons. Feeling hurt and rejected by their father, the ten older sons became angry and vindictive toward their younger brother.

"Israel [Jacob] loved Joseph more than any of his other sons, because he had been born to him in his old age; and he made a richly ornamented robe for him. When

his brothers saw that their father loved him more than any of them, they hated him and could not speak a kind word to him." (Genesis 37:3–4)

2 INJUSTICE: Your right is violated.[17]

Everyone has a knowledge of right and wrong, fair and unfair, just and *unjust*. When you perceive an *injustice* has occurred to you or to others (especially to those you love), you may feel angry. If you hold on to the offense, the unresolved anger can begin to take root in your heart.

BIBLICAL EXAMPLE: King Saul
King Saul's *unjust* treatment of David evoked Jonathan's anger. Jonathan, son of Saul, heard his own father pronounce a death sentence on his dear friend David.

"'Why should he be put to death? What has he done?' Jonathan asked his father. But Saul hurled his spear at him to kill him [Jonathan]. Then Jonathan knew that his father intended to kill David. Jonathan got up from the table in fierce anger." (1 Samuel 20:32–34)

3 FEAR: Your future is threatened.[18]

Everyone is created with a God-given inner need for *security*.[19] When you begin to worry, feel threatened, or get angry because of a change in circumstances, you may be responding to *fear*. A fearful heart reveals a lack of trust in God's perfect plan for your life.

BIBLICAL EXAMPLE: King Saul
Saul became angry because of David's many successes on the battlefield. (Read 1 Samuel 18:5–15, 28–29.) He was threatened by David's popularity and *feared* he would lose his kingdom.

"Saul was very angry ... 'They have credited David with tens of thousands,' he thought, 'but me with only thousands.' ... Saul was afraid of David, because the Lord was with David but had left Saul."
(1 Samuel 18:8, 12)

4 FRUSTRATION: Your performance is not accepted.[20]

Everyone has a God-given inner need for *significance*.[21] When your efforts are thwarted or do not meet your own personal expectations, your sense of significance can be threatened. *Frustration* over unmet expectations of yourself or of others is a major source of anger.

BIBLICAL EXAMPLE: Cain

Both Cain and Abel brought offerings to God, but Cain's offering was clearly unacceptable. Cain had chosen to offer what he himself wanted to give rather than what God said was right and acceptable. When Cain's self-effort was rejected, his *frustration* led to anger, and his anger led to the murder of his own brother.

"In the course of time Cain brought some of the fruits of the soil as an offering to the LORD. But Abel brought fat portions from some of the firstborn of his flock. The LORD looked with favor on Abel and his offering, but on Cain and his offering he did not look with favor. So Cain was very angry, and his face was downcast. ... Now Cain said to his brother Abel, 'Let's go out to the field.' And while they were in the field, Cain attacked his brother Abel and killed him."
(Genesis 4:3–5, 8)

Anger and Inappropriate Anger

QUESTION: "What does God want me to do about my inappropriate anger?"[22]

ANSWER: God wants you to examine the true source of your anger. Is it *hurt, injustice, fear, frustration,* or a combination of these? Then evaluate whether you are using anger to try to get your inner need for love, for significance, or for security met.

▶ Have you been **hurt** by rejection or someone's unkind words? If so, ask…

Am I using anger to try to intimidate or coerce someone to remain in a relationship with me?

▶ Have you been a victim of an **unjust** situation where you felt powerless? If so, ask…

Am I using angry, accusatory words to cause someone to feel guilty and obligated to me?

▶ Have you been **afraid** because of a situation you can't control? If so, ask…

Am I using anger to overpower and control someone in order to get my way?

▶ Have you been **frustrated** because of something you can't do? If so, ask…

Am I using angry threats and shaming words to manipulate someone to meet my demands?

In searching your heart, decide that you will not use anger to try to get your needs met. Instead, repent and no longer look to others to meet your needs. Enter into a deeper dependence on the Lord to meet these God-given needs, because…

"The LORD will guide you always; he will satisfy

your needs in a sun-scorched land and will
strengthen your frame. You will be like a
well-watered garden, like a spring whose waters
never fail." (Isaiah 58:11)

WHAT CAUSES a Sudden Increase in Anger Intensity?

When most people envision a raging inferno, they imagine a wild forest fire or rows of homes engulfed by flames. But in 1999 an entirely different kind of fire broke out in North Delta, Canada, as a roaring fire filled 250,000 cubic yards in a landfill.

The fire was caused by tons upon tons of loosely piled waste, which created a single, 50-foot column deposited in a way that violated two important permit requirements.

The local fire department responded to the North Delta landfill fire with several pumper trucks that worked around the clock for 24 hours to put the fire out—*or so they thought*.

But a few days later the fire actually intensified when flames broke out on the steep face of the landfill following a 50-yard by 100-yard sinkhole that fell about 10 feet where the flames had originally been concentrated.[23]

Anger can also intensify, seemingly coming out of nowhere, warranting close examination of its cause.

Although a person's ways of expressing anger may change slightly over time, they seldom change dramatically. A dramatic change would not be typical. When there is a major change, there is also a major cause.

If someone is uncharacteristically impatient, irritable, or provoked, be aware that *changes in mood and behavior can result from ...*

▶ **Drug abuse** (steroids, cocaine)

▶ **Medications** (certain antidepressants)

▶ **Head injury** (sports, fall, car accident)

▶ **Chemical deficiencies** (hormonal imbalances)

▶ **Illness or disease** (brain tumor, brain cancer)

▶ **Physical stress and emotional trauma**
   (post-traumatic stress disorder)

▶ **Spiritual rebellion** (blatant refusal to acknowledge, worship, or obey God)

Sudden changes of behavior warrant a close examination as to what could be a physical cause, especially in the brain. Be prudent—don't judge too quickly—and seek knowledge because ...

"Every prudent man acts out of knowledge,
but a fool exposes his folly."
(Proverbs 13:16)

Anger and Depression

QUESTION: "Can depression be caused by anger?"

ANSWER: Yes. If you have anger but do not process and release it, over time your anger can turn inward, which often produces depression. But there are other causes of depression as well:

▶ **Clinical depression** can result when the physical body does not naturally produce essential mood-elevating chemicals.

▶ **Chemical depression** can develop when medications interfere with the production of certain neurotransmitters.

▶ **Postpartum depression** occurs in some mothers when their hormone levels drop following the birth of their babies.

▶ **Situational depression** is caused by painful situations in which the heart is grieved (for example, death of a loved one, divorce, job loss).

Regardless of the cause of a person's depression, hope and praise are effective antidotes.

> "Why are you downcast, O my soul? Why so disturbed within me? Put your hope in God, for I will yet praise him, my Savior and my God."
> (Psalm 42:11)

DO EXPECTATIONS Lead to Anger?

When it comes to anger, *unrealistic expectations* can be harmful—much like trying to put out a fire with gasoline. When it came to battling the Canadian landfill blaze, any expectation of quickly extinguishing the fire proved futile.

A thick haze of smoke choked out the fresh air and sunlight for miles. Of greater concern was a gas pipeline dangerously close to the billowing flames, posing a serious threat to life and property. Even the water supply was threatened by the pooling of leachate (the liquid drainage from the landfill).

After consulting with firefighting specialists, authorities decided to excavate the burning material

and transport it to another area where it could be fully immersed in water.[24]

How easy to adopt the unrealistic expectation that we have the power to determine what people should do or how situations *should* be. "My destiny should be *this*; therefore, people should do *that*." Typically, we pray and *expect* God to do everything we ask. We want to be the fire chief, when in reality He alone is the One in charge.

The primary problem with unrealistic expectations centers around the simple word "pride." We would be wise to ask the Lord, "Do I act as though I am the center of my world and everything revolves around me?" The Bible describes angry reactions resulting from unmet expectations.

"What causes fights and quarrels among you? Don't they come from your desires that battle within you? You want something but don't get it. You kill and covet, but you cannot have what you want. You quarrel and fight. You do not have, because you do not ask God. When you ask, you do not receive, because you ask with wrong motives, that you may spend what you get on your pleasures. ... 'God opposes the proud but gives grace to the humble.'" (James 4:1–3, 6)

Unrealistic Expectations

Anger toward circumstances

"I expected good things would always come my way —but my life is clearly not what I had expected."

Anger toward others

"I expected you to always be here for me, to love and support me—but now I feel alone and lonely."

Anger toward yourself

"I expected to always excel—but now I am struggling and feel like a failure."

Anger toward God

"I expected God to protect me from pain and provide health and wealth as He promised—but He hasn't answered my prayers."

The more we expect God and people to do what we want, the angrier we become when they fail us. Truth is, the more we try to control others, the more control we give them over ourselves. The more demands we put on others, *the more power we give them* to anger us. Instead, we need to humble ourselves and submit to God's sovereignty over our lives and over the lives of others. We need to leave our desires and our destiny in His hands—where they rightly belong.

The Bible says we are to lay our hopes and expectations before the Lord and allow Him to determine what we should receive.

> "Find rest, O my soul, in God alone; my hope comes from him." (Psalm 62:5)

Anger over Unrealistic Expectations

QUESTION: "Since the Bible says, 'Ask and you will receive,' I was told that all I had to do was name and claim what I wanted—in Jesus' name. If I would sincerely 'believe,' I could expect to 'receive,' which clearly hasn't happened! I'm angry with God. Why hasn't He answered my prayers?"

ANSWER: Your anger at God is based on *unrealistic expectations*. While you were completely sincere,

those who taught you this expectation were sincerely wrong. The *Name It-Claim It* theology is not biblical.

When you look at the *whole counsel of God*—reading all Scriptures on the same subject in their accurate context—you will see that the "believe and receive" doctrine doesn't measure up as biblically accurate.

▶ Consider the apostle Paul, whose pedigree was impressive, yet he knew what it was to lack health and wealth. Although 100% in the will of God, he was also weak and "*in want.*" He said, "*I know what it is to be in need, and I know what it is to have plenty. I have learned the secret of being content in any and every situation, whether well fed or hungry, whether living in plenty or in want. I can do everything through him who gives me strength.*" (Philippians 4:12–13)

▶ Jesus tells us that whatever we ask in faith, we will receive: "*I tell you, whatever you ask for in prayer, believe that you have received it, and it will be yours*" (Mark 11:24). At face value, this verse appears to back up the belief that God will give us whatever we ask—as long as we believe, we will receive it. Yet the apostle John gives us clarification: If your desire conforms to God's will, He will look upon your request with favor and allow it to come to pass. The Bible says …

> "If we ask anything according to his will, he hears us. And … we know that we have what we asked of him."
> (1 John 5:14–15)

QUESTION: "How can I handle my anger over the losses in my life?"

ANSWER: When you experience significant loss in your life, you will go through a time of grieving.

▶ **Admit your feelings**—your hurt, sense of injustice, fear, or frustration.

▶ **Release to God** all the pain you feel, along with the situations beyond your control.

▶ **Trust God** to give you the grace and insight to deal constructively with each loss.

▶ **Release your expectation** that life must go your way.

Pray, "Lord, thank You for being sovereign over my life. Whatever it takes, I want to respond to You with a heart of gratitude and to accept the unchangeable circumstances in my life. I choose to stop making myself and those around me miserable by being angry over something none of us can change. Instead, I thank You for what You are going to teach me through this loss. And thank You for Your promise that somehow You are going to use this loss for good. In Your holy name I pray, Amen."

Repeatedly remind yourself to …

"Give thanks in all circumstances, for this is
God's will for you in Christ Jesus."
(1 Thessalonians 5:18)

The root cause of extended anger is typically based on a "wrong" premise about "rights." The root cause of the nearly catastrophic Canadian landfill blaze was also based on a wrong premise about rights: Unscrupulous business owners chose to operate their landfill in their own illegitimate way rather than yielding to the official permit requirements for landfills.[25]

When we feel that our real or perceived "rights" have been violated, we can easily respond with anger.[26] But what are our legitimate rights? One person would answer, "Happiness." Another would say, "Freedom to live life my way."

Yet this was not the mind-set of Jesus. He yielded His rights to His heavenly Father. Based on the Bible, *we have the right to live in the light of God's will as revealed in His Word.* Other than that, we are to yield our rights to the Lord and let Him have His way in our hearts. We are told to ...

> "Trust in the Lord with all your heart and lean not on your own understanding; in all your ways acknowledge him, and he will make your paths straight." (Proverbs 3:5–6)

▶ WRONG BELIEF

"When I am hurt, fearful, frustrated, or treated unfairly, *I have the right* to be angry until the situation changes. It is only natural for me to be angry about the disappointments in my life and to express my anger in whatever way I choose."

▶ RIGHT BELIEF

"Since I have trusted Christ with my life and

have yielded my rights to Him, I choose not to be controlled by anger. My human disappointments are now God's appointments to increase my faith and develop His character in me." The Bible says …

"Now for a little while you may have had to suffer grief in all kinds of trials. These have come so that your faith—of greater worth than gold, which perishes even though refined by fire —may be proved genuine" (1 Peter 1:6–7).

Do You Want to Know God's Plan for Your Life and for Controlling Your Anger?

No one wants to be thought of as "out-of-control." No one wants to live with anger that is out of control. Yet, so often, someone will say, "I've really tried to control my anger, but for some reason, I just can't."

If that someone is you, it could be that the Lord is saying, "I know you can't—but I can. I can provide you the control you need—My supernatural power can be at work in your weakness—recognize My authority over you and give Me control of your life. I can change you from the inside out."

Do you need a real change in your life? If so, there are four truths you need to know in order to have a changed life.

#1 God's Purpose for You is *Salvation.*

What was God's motivation in sending Jesus Christ to earth?

To express His love for you by saving you! The Bible says …

"God so loved the world that he gave his one and only

Son, that whoever believes in him shall not perish but have eternal life. For God did not send his Son into the world to condemn the world, but to save the world through him." (John 3:16–17)

What was Jesus' purpose in coming to earth?

To forgive your sins, to empower you to have victory over sin—including anger—and to enable you to live a fulfilled life!

Jesus said, *"I have come that they may have life, and that they may have it more abundantly."* (John 10:10 NKJV)

#2 Your Problem is *Sin*.

What exactly is sin?

Sin is living independently of God's standard—knowing what is right, but choosing what is wrong. The Bible says ...

"Anyone, then, who knows the good he ought to do and doesn't do it, sins." (James 4:17)

What is the major consequence of sin?

Spiritual death, eternal separation from God. Scripture states ...

"Your iniquities [sins] have separated you from your God ... The wages of sin is death, but the gift of God is eternal life in Christ Jesus our Lord." (Isaiah 59:2; Romans 6:23)

#3 God's Provision for You is the *Savior*.

Can anything remove the penalty for sin?

Yes! Jesus died on the cross to personally pay the

penalty for your sins. The Bible says ...

"God demonstrates his own love for us in this: While we were still sinners, Christ died for us." (Romans 5:8)

What is the solution to being separated from God?

Belief in (entrusting your life to) Jesus Christ as the only way to God the Father. Jesus says ...

"I am the way and the truth and the life. No one comes to the Father except through me. ... Believe in the Lord Jesus, and you will be saved." (John 14:6; Acts 16:31)

#4 Your Part is *Surrender*.

Give Christ control of your life—entrusting yourself to Him.

"Jesus said to his disciples, 'If anyone would come after me, he must deny himself and take up his cross [die to your own self-rule] and follow me. For whoever wants to save his life will lose it, but whoever loses his life for me will find it. What good will it be for a man if he gains the whole world, yet forfeits his soul?'" (Matthew 16:24–26)

Place your faith in (rely on) Jesus Christ as your personal Lord and Savior and reject your "good works" as a means of earning God's approval.

"It is by grace you have been saved, through faith—and this not from yourselves, it is the gift of God—not by works, so that no one can boast." (Ephesians 2:8–9)

The moment you choose to receive Jesus as your Lord and Savior—entrusting your life to Him—He comes

to live inside you. Then He gives you His power to live the fulfilled life God has planned for you. If you want to be fully forgiven by God and become the person God created you to be, you can tell Him in a simple, heartfelt prayer like this:

PRAYER OF SALVATION

"God, I want a real relationship with You.
I admit that many times I've chosen to go
my own way instead of Your way.
Please forgive me for my sins.
Jesus, thank You for dying on the cross
to pay the penalty for my sins.
Come into my life to be
my Lord and my Savior.
Change me from the inside out and make me
the person You created me to be.
In Your holy name I pray. Amen."

What Can You Expect Now?

If you sincerely prayed this prayer, look at what God says!

"His divine power has given us everything we need
for life and godliness through our knowledge of him
who called us by his own glory and goodness. Through
these he has given us his very great and precious
promises, so that through them you may participate
in the divine nature and escape the corruption in the
world caused by evil desires." (2 Peter 1:3–4)

STEPS TO SOLUTION

FRUSTRATION IGNITES ANGER

On that hot, dry day, Moses' frustration reached a boiling point. He had led more than a million of his people through the vast desert. But for all of his efforts, they continually complained, criticizing his leadership and condemning him for their plight: *"If only we had died when our brothers fell dead! ... Why did you bring us up out of Egypt to this terrible place?"* (Numbers 20:3–5)

Now once again, they had no water. Earlier in their journey, God had miraculously provided water by instructing Moses to strike a particular rock with his staff. When Moses obeyed, a stream of water—enough for all of Israel—poured out of the rock. (See Exodus 17:1–6.)

Now, at this point, God intended to perform a similar miracle, but He told Moses to simply speak to—not strike—a certain rock. However, Moses was so frustrated with the people that his anger boiled over the edge. Rather than speaking to the rock, he forcefully struck the rock—not once, but twice. Gushing water is what God intended—not gushing anger. As a result, God disciplined His chosen leader by not allowing him to lead His chosen people into the Promised Land. (See Numbers 20:1–12.)

At times, are you like Moses? Do you ever allow injustice, hurt, fear, or frustration to make you furious, for which you receive a painful repercussion? If so, what should you do when you get angry? The Bible says...

"Refrain from anger and turn from wrath;
do not fret—it leads only to evil."
(Psalm 37:8)

HOW TO Measure the Amount of Your Anger

Before firefighters respond to any alarm, they measure the intensity of the emergency and then rally the necessary resources.

A one-alarm fire is considered the least serious, usually dispatching to the scene two pumper trucks, a rescue unit, a ladder truck, and a supervising chief. A two-alarm fire doubles the response of a one-alarm call.

In situations considered three-alarm to five-alarm fires, besides adding more of the above, trucks storing oxygen and area lighting are also sent to the scene, along with a crew for media relations and food and water replenishments for firefighters.

Similar to the standard procedure of firefighters, taking the time to measure your anger is necessary for knowing how to put the fire of anger out.

Have you seriously thought about *how much* anger you are holding inside your heart and *toward whom* you feel angry? See the pie-shaped outline on the following page. Divide the pie into segments and put a specific name inside each segment to represent the amount of anger you feel toward the different people in your life (past or present). (See the example which shows general categories.[27])

As you think about your own anger, consider what the Bible says:

"Man's anger does not bring about
the righteous life that God desires." (James 1:20)

Example:

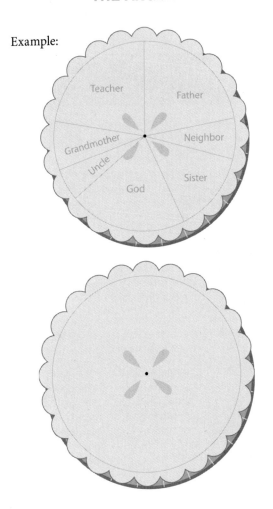

Fire investigators have the responsibility of analyzing the aftermath of a fire to determine where the fire started, what started it, and why it got out of control. The goal is to formulate a plan to prevent such fires from getting started in the future and to control and extinguish them should they break out again. Likewise, analyzing your anger will help you determine where it started, what started it, and why it got out of control, but also how to prevent it and how to control it should it break out again.

To better understand your anger, each time you feel angry, stop and ask yourself key thought-provoking questions. Analyzing your thoughts and actions can help you move from being controlled by your anger to benefiting from your anger. As you practice patience and gain understanding, you will be able to use your anger for God's purpose, which, in turn, will prevent foolish displays of anger you later regret.

> "A patient man has great understanding,
> but a quick-tempered man displays folly."
> (Proverbs 14:29)

The Anger Quiz

As you answer each question, think for a moment and answer as honestly as you can.

▶ What triggers your anger?

▶ How do you generally express your anger?

▶ What do you desire when you are angry?

▶ Is the way you express your anger working for you? Do you get what you desire?

▶ Do you ever lose control of your anger? If so, when was the last time you did, and what happened?

▶ Are you able to calm your anger? If so, what do you do?

▶ Have you allowed your anger to escalate? If so, what happened?

▶ Is your anger harming your relationships? If so, how?

▶ Has your anger ever caused any health problems? If so, what?

▶ Do others point out your anger even if you don't see it? If so, when, and what do they say?

▶ Does your anger ever become physical? If so, how and how often?

▶ When you get angry, how safe do you feel?

▶ When you get angry, how safe do others feel?

▶ Did anyone in your childhood home have an anger problem? If so, who, and how were you impacted back then?

▶ As a child, how did you feel when you were on the receiving end of someone's anger?

▶ Do you think anger from your childhood could still be impacting you today? If so, how?

▶ Do you have difficulty forgiving those toward whom you have anger? If so, explain.

▶ Do you have someone wise to talk with about your anger?

▶ Do you ever pray about your anger? If so, what do you pray?

▶ What is your view of God in the midst of angering situations?

▶ How do you think you should respond to God when you feel angry?

▶ How do you think you should respond to others when you feel angry?

▶ What can you learn from a recent anger problem that will help you better handle your anger in the future?

When you honestly analyze your anger, you are taking the first step toward controlling your temper rather than letting your temper control you.

> "Better a patient man than a warrior,
> a man who controls his temper
> than one who takes a city."
> (Proverbs 16:32)

When a raging, fiery inferno engulfs a home with a tragic loss of life, the gut-wrenching pain can be punctuated by a finger pointing upward. However, harboring anger toward God for our heartaches is like blaming our losses on the fire chief—the one who has devoted his entire life to helping, not hurting, us.

No one escapes hurt and pain in life—*no one*. During catastrophic times, the promise you are to cling to is that your loving God is unfolding His perfect plan for your life, and He uses *all* circumstances to accomplish His purposes—*even the painful ones*.

Have you ever blamed God for the pain and heartache in your life? Have you pointed a condemning finger and pronounced judgment on Him because He has not stopped evil or suffering?

In the Bible, a man named Job seriously questioned God—so much so that we can hear anger in his bitter complaint: *"Even today my complaint is bitter; his [God's] hand is heavy in spite of my groaning. If only I knew where to find him; if only I could go to his dwelling! I would state my case before him and fill my mouth with arguments."* (Job 23:2–4)

But is anger toward God justifiable? While He understands our anger, notice how He sets the record straight by answering Job with these words: *"Who is this that darkens my counsel with words without knowledge? ... Will the one who contends with the Almighty correct him? ... Would you discredit my justice? Would you condemn me to justify yourself?"* (Job 38:2; 40:2, 8)

What is the answer to intense anger against God? Can it be resolved? And if so, how? The sure way to resolve your anger toward God is to gain a full understanding of the character, purpose, and plan of God.

Resolving Anger toward God

▶ **Know God's Character.**

- **He is just.** *"He is the Rock, his works are perfect, and all his ways are just. A faithful God who does no wrong, upright and just is he."* (Deut. 32:4)

- **His ways are just.** *"Just and true are your ways, King of the ages."* (Revelation 15:3)

- **He is love.** *"God is love."* (1 John 4:8)

- **He loves.** *"We love because he first loved us."* (1 John 4:19)

▶ **Know God's Purposes.**

- **He brings good out of evil.** *"We know that in all things God works for the good of those who love him."* (Romans 8:28)

- **He turns your sorrow into joy.** *"You turned my wailing into dancing; you removed my sackcloth and clothed me with joy."* (Psalm 30:11)

- **He uses your suffering** to produce perseverance, character, and hope. *"We also rejoice in our sufferings, because we know that suffering produces perseverance; perseverance, character; and character, hope. And hope does not disappoint us, because God has poured out his love into our hearts."* (Romans 5:3–5)

- **He uses your troubles** to teach you compassion. *"The Father of compassion and the God of all*

*comfort ... comforts us in all our troubles, so
that we can comfort those in any trouble with the
comfort we ourselves have received from God.*"
(2 Corinthians 1:3–4)

▶ **Know God's Plan.**

- **He will grant eternal life to you** and all who
  entrust their lives to Christ. "*My Father's will is
  that everyone who looks to the Son and believes in
  him shall have eternal life, and I will raise him up
  at the last day.*" (John 6:40)

- **He will bless you** if you persevere under trial.
  "*Blessed is the man who perseveres under trial.*"
  (James 1:12)

- **He will bring His righteous judgment** on those
  who are evil. "*The Lord knows how to rescue godly
  men from trials and to hold the unrighteous for the
  day of judgment.*" (2 Peter 2:9)

- **He will, one day, make everything new** for His
  true believers. "*The dwelling of God is with men,
  and he will live with them. They will be his people,
  and God himself will be with them and be their
  God. He will wipe every tear from their eyes. There
  will be no more death or mourning or crying or
  pain, for the old order of things has passed away.*"
  (Revelation 21:3–4)

Job, who at one time had anger toward God, ultimately
realized that he had misplaced anger. With deepest
remorse, he admitted his wrong.

"I know that you can do all things; no plan of
yours can be thwarted. ...My ears had heard of
you but now my eyes have seen you. Therefore I
despise myself and repent in dust and ashes."
(Job 42:2, 5–6)

Anger That God Allows Evil

QUESTION: "I'm angry at God for allowing bad people to cause so much pain. Since God had the power to create the world, why doesn't He stop evil in the world?"

ANSWER: God allows evil because He allows people to exercise "free will."

▶ God did not create us to be robots with no choice to do anything except what the Creator has programmed.

▶ He created us to be "free agent" human beings who have choice over what we think, say, and do. We can't have it both ways, in that God allows us freedom but we can't do anything wrong. That's not freedom!

If you have read the last chapter of the book of Revelation, you know that God has appointed a time in the future when He will put an end to evil and suffering.

▶ The bad news is that until then, evil will always be in opposition to good and will seek to harm and destroy those who do good.

▶ But the good news is that God always uses harmful experiences to accomplish His purposes. He did so in the life of Joseph, whose evil brothers sold him into slavery. Years later when the frightened brothers came face-to-face with him—by then prime minister of Egypt, who had saved both the Egyptians and the Hebrews from famine—Joseph said ...

"Don't be afraid. Am I in the place of God? You

intended to harm me, but God intended it for
good to accomplish what is now being done, the
saving of many lives." (Genesis 50:19–20)

HOW TO Resolve Your Past Anger

We've all seen pictures of people walking on hot
coals, appearing to defy nature by taking a short, yet
potentially scorching, journey with feet unscathed.
It's no mystery that the "trick" to salvaging the soles
is to move fast, never lingering long enough for the
fiery coals to begin burning skin. If for some reason
the treacherous trek is prolonged, *pain and injury* will
ensue.

Failure to resolve past anger operates in much the
same way. The longer it resides in your heart, the more
painful and injurious it is for you and for others. That's
because unresolved anger produces bitterness. And
bitterness is like a bed of hidden coals burning deep
wounds into your soul and spirit, making rubble of
your relationships. This thief of emotion snatches joy
from your heart and steals peace from your spirit—it
even robs your mind of reason.

"When my heart was grieved and my spirit
embittered, I was senseless and ignorant; I was
a brute beast before you." (Psalm 73:21–22)

Putting Away Past Anger

REALIZE Your Unresolved Anger.

▶ **Admit** you have harbored anger in your heart and
confess it as sin.

▶ **Ask** God to reveal all of your unresolved anger.

▶ **Admit** to a wise, nonjudgmental friend or counselor that you have buried anger.

▶ **Ask** God to help you see your sin as He sees your sin.

Say to the Lord, *"I confess my iniquity; I am troubled by my sin."* (Psalm 38:18)

REVISIT Your Root Feelings.

▶ Did you **feel hurt:** rejected, betrayed, unloved, ignored?

▶ Did you **experience injustice:** cheated, wronged, maligned, attacked?

▶ Did you **feel fearful:** threatened, insecure, out-of-control, powerless?

▶ Did you **feel frustrated:** inadequate, inferior, hindered, controlled?

Pray to the Lord, *"Search me, O God, and know my heart; test me and know my anxious thoughts. See if there is any offensive way in me, and lead me in the way everlasting."* (Psalm 139:23–24)

RELEASE Your Rights Regarding the Offense.

▶ **Release** your right to hear "I'm sorry" for the offense.

▶ **Release** your right to dwell on the offense.

▶ **Release** your right to hold on to the offense.

▶ **Release** your right to keep bringing up the offense.

Remember, *"He who covers over an offense promotes love, but whoever repeats the matter separates close friends."* (Proverbs 17:9)

RECOGNIZE Your Need to Forgive.

▶ **Make** a list of each of your hurts—release each one to God.

▶ **Pray** for those who persecute you—for whatever is broken in them.

▶ **Give** your desire for revenge to God—do not strike back or retaliate.

▶ **Release** those who have hurt you into the hands of God—forgive as God forgave you!

Be faithful to, *"Bear with each other and forgive whatever grievances you may have against one another. Forgive as the Lord forgave you."* (Col. 3:13)

REJOICE in God's Purpose for Allowing Your Pain.

▶ **Thank God** for the ways He will use this trial in your life—truly for your good.

▶ **Thank God** for how He will use your resolved anger for the good of others.

▶ **Thank God** for His promise to restore you after a time of suffering.

▶ **Thank God** for His promise to use all the pain to make you strong, firm, and steadfast.

Give thanks that, *"The God of all grace, who called you to his eternal glory in Christ, after you have suffered a little while, will himself restore you and make you strong, firm and steadfast."* (1 Peter 5:10)

RESTORE the Relationship When Appropriate.

(Note: Sometimes reconciliation is not appropriate,

such as with an unrepentant abuser or between two people involved in an adulterous affair.)

▶ **Confess your anger** both to God and to the person with whom you have resisted or have not wanted reconciliation.

Write out the confession first to get the wording just right.

"I realize I've been wrong in holding on to my anger and refusing to allow God to restore our relationship. I'm deeply sorry. Will you forgive me?"

▶ **Keep the encounter** free of anger and accusatory statements.

Instead of "You did _____." statements, use "I felt (sad, hurt, devastated, etc.) when (event) happened."

▶ **State your desire** for a renewed reconciliation within a right relationship.

"I sincerely want us to have the best relationship possible—a healthy, supportive, positive relationship that is right in God's sight. Is that what you desire?"

Realize it is Jesus who said, *"I tell you that anyone who is angry with his brother will be subject to judgment. ... Therefore, if you are offering your gift at the altar and there remember that your brother has something against you, leave your gift there in front of the altar. First go and be reconciled to your brother; then come and offer your gift."* (Matthew 5:22–24)

RECEIVE God's Love for You Personally.

▶ **Personalize** Bible verses that reveal God's love for you:

Lord, thank you for saying to me, *"I have loved you with an everlasting love."* (Jeremiah 31:3)

God, *"Because of [your] great love [I am] not consumed, for [your] compassions never fail. They are new every morning; great is your faithfulness."* (Lamentations 3:22–23)

▶ **Read** these Scriptures daily for eight weeks:

"The LORD's unfailing love surrounds the man who trusts in him. … I will sing of the Lord's great love forever … The LORD's love is with those who fear him [revere him]" (Psalm 32:10; 89:1; 103:17)

▶ **Rely** on the Lord to meet your inner needs for love, significance, and security: [29]

Lord, *"I trust in your unfailing love; my heart rejoices in your salvation."* (Psalm 13:5)

▶ **Thank God** each day for His unconditional love:

Lord, *"How great is the love [you have] lavished on [me], that [I] should be called [a child] of God!"* (1 John 3:1)

Pray with the apostle Paul, *"That you, being rooted and established in love, may have power, together with all the saints, to grasp how wide and long and high and deep is the love of Christ, and to know this love that surpasses knowledge—that you may be filled to the measure of all the fullness of God."* (Ephesians 3:17–19)

REFLECT Christ's Love.

▶ **Reflect the love of Jesus by praying** for every person who hurts or angers you.

"Lord, may **my heart** be a reflection of Your heart."

"Lord, may **my mind** be an expression of Your mind."

"Lord, may **my will** be an illustration of Your will."

"Lord, may **my love** be a demonstration of Your love."

Jesus gave this proclamation to His disciples and, therefore, to us. *"A new command I give you: Love one another. As I have loved you, so you must love one another. By this all men will know that you are my disciples, if you love one another."* (John 13:34–35)

Anger and Reconciliation?[30]

QUESTION: "I feel angry at the thought of having to reconcile with someone I trusted—someone who played me for a fool. With no remorse, no repentance, no restitution, he remains untrustworthy, so how can I forgive and be reconciled?"

ANSWER: Forgiveness is not the same as reconciliation. Forgiveness focuses on the offense, whereas reconciliation focuses on the relationship. Forgiveness requires no relationship. However, reconciliation requires a relationship in which two people, in agreement, are walking together toward the same goal. The Bible says ...

"Do two walk together unless they have agreed to do so?" (Amos 3:3)

▶ **Forgiveness** can be given by one person.

Reconciliation requires at least two people.

63

▶ **Forgiveness** is extended in one direction.

Reconciliation is reciprocal, involving a two-way direction.

▶ **Forgiveness** is a decision to release the offender.

Reconciliation is the effort to rejoin the offender.

▶ **Forgiveness** involves a change in thinking about the offender.

Reconciliation involves a change in behavior by the offender.

▶ **Forgiveness** is a free gift to the one who has broken trust.

Reconciliation is a restored relationship based on restored trust.

▶ **Forgiveness** is extended even if it is never, ever earned.

Reconciliation is offered to the offender because it has been earned.

▶ **Forgiveness** is unconditional, regardless of a lack of repentance.

Reconciliation is conditional and is based on repentance.

You can forgive your offender, but you cannot reconcile with someone who remains unchanged. As the Scripture instructs, *"Do not make friends with a hot-tempered man, do not associate with one easily angered."* (Proverbs 22:24)

Ask a group of 5-year-old boys what they want to be when they grow up and the odds are high that more than one will say a fireman. Adults smile at the endearing aspiration, knowing full well the odds are just as high that the little boys standing before them probably won't actually become *firefighters*.

The struggles and hurts of life have a way of shattering the innocence of youth, and the anger experienced perhaps by even a 5-year-old boy can affect him as a 50-year-old man if it is not resolved. Often a direct connection can be found between *present* pain and anger and *past* pain and anger, dating even all the way back to early childhood. Many of us assume when we reach adulthood, our childhood pain will magically disappear and no longer affect us. *Surely, the years have suffocated the last smoldering ember*, we reason. However, this disappearing act doesn't "just happen." We must recognize our pain from the past and resolve it, because ...

> "The good man brings good things out of the good stored up in him, and the evil man brings evil things out of the evil stored up in him."
> (Matthew 12:35)

Resolving Childhood Hurts

The next time anger wells up in your heart, ask yourself ...

▶ "Am I feeling *hurt*?"

EXAMPLE: "The dearest person in my life is rejecting me."

▶ "Did I ever have these same feelings when I was a child?"

EXAMPLE: "My father basically ignored me and strongly favored my brother."

▶ "How did I feel when my father ignored me?"

EXAMPLE: "I felt sad, mad, and rejected."

▶ "How did I express my anger?"

EXAMPLE: "I picked on my brother and was mean to him."

Face the anger still residing in your heart because of childhood hurts ...

▶ Ask God to reveal buried hurts from your childhood.

▶ Ask close family members and friends to describe what situations seem to hurt you and make you angry.

▶ Acknowledge that your prolonged, unresolved anger over past hurts is wrong, even if you think it is justified.

▶ Take personal responsibility to overcome your childhood hurts.

▶ Surrender your hurtful childhood experiences and feelings to God.

▶ Ask forgiveness from those whom you have hurt or offended.

▶ Forgive and pray for those who have hurt you.

▶ Pray for God to purge you of your hurtful ways and fill you with His unconditional love for others.

If your heart yearns for love and acceptance, remember ...

▶ Psalm 66:20—*"Praise be to God, who has not rejected my prayer or withheld his love from me!"*

▶ Psalm 32:10—*"Many are the woes of the wicked, but the LORD's unfailing love surrounds the man who trusts in him."*

▶ Psalm 36:7—*"How priceless is your unfailing love! Both high and low among men find refuge in the shadow of your wings."*

▶ 1 John 4:9–10—*"This is how God showed his love among us: He sent his one and only Son into the world that we might live through him. This is love: not that we loved God, but that he loved us and sent his Son as an atoning sacrifice for our sins."*

Resolving Childhood Injustices

The next time you feel the surge of anger over a particular situation, ask yourself ...

▶ "Am I feeling a sense of injustice?"

   EXAMPLE: "The person I'm dating mistreats me."

▶ "Did I ever have these same feelings in my childhood?"

   EXAMPLE: "Yes. When my father abused my mother, my brother, and me."

▶ "How did I feel when my father abused all of us?"

   EXAMPLE: "I felt angry and powerless to stop it."

▶ "How did I express my anger?"

   EXAMPLE: "I bullied other kids."

Face your anger from the past and begin to see how your present anger is connected to the injustices you experienced in childhood. ...

▶ Ask God to reveal all unresolved feelings over the injustices you experienced as a child.

▶ Ask your close family members and friends how they know when you are angry over an injustice.

▶ Acknowledge that your feelings of injustice may be directed toward God.

▶ Take personal responsibility for your feelings of anger at injustice.

▶ Release your anger to God over past injustices and replace the anger with God's peace.

▶ Ask forgiveness from anyone you have treated unjustly.

▶ Forgive and pray for those who have been unjust toward you.

▶ Meditate on how God can use your awareness of injustices committed against you and against others for good.

If your anger is rooted in unjust treatment, and you are committed to justice, remember ...

▶ Psalm 9:16—*"The LORD is known by his justice."*

▶ Luke 18:7—*"Will not God bring about justice for his chosen ones, who cry out to him day and night? Will he keep putting them off?"*

▶ 2 Thessalonians 1:6–7—*"God is just: He will pay back trouble to those who trouble you and give relief to you who are troubled, and to us as well."*

▶ Psalm 37:6—"*He will make your righteousness shine like the dawn, the justice of your cause like the noonday sun.*"

Resolving Childhood Frustrations

The next time you feel anger when your personal efforts are stymied or unaccepted by others, ask yourself…

▶ "Am I feeling *frustrated*?"

EXAMPLE: "My associate made negative remarks about my speech at our business luncheon."

▶ "Did I ever have these same feelings in my childhood?"

EXAMPLE: "Yes. When my parents expected me to behave perfectly and to not express my true feelings."

▶ "How did I feel when my parents had these expectations?"

EXAMPLE: "I felt like they accepted me only when my behavior was acceptable, so I ended up feeling angry and insecure all the time."

▶ "How did I express my anger?"

EXAMPLE: "I got mad at them and at myself and would bang my head a lot or scratch my arms."

Face your past frustrations from childhood and realize that not measuring up to your own or someone else's standards indicates performance-based acceptance and can be a major source of anger.

▶ Ask God to reveal the buried anger you have

toward your parents or others in your past who frustrated you by accepting you only on the basis of your performance.

▶ Ask yourself …

- "Do I set unrealistic standards for myself?"
- "Do I tend to stuff my anger?"
- "Do I need to control people and circumstances?"
- "Am I a caretaker?"
- "Am I a perfectionist?"
- "Am I a procrastinator?"
- "Am I a people pleaser?"
- "Am I a workaholic?"

▶ Ask your family and close friends how they know when you are frustrated.

▶ Understand that frustration is only a nice-sounding word for the anger that deeply damages your self-worth and sense of significance.

▶ Understand that it takes concentrated commitment and great effort to uncover deeply buried frustrations and root them out of your life.

▶ Realize you can never earn God's love, but He loves you unconditionally.

▶ Allow yourself to feel your anger at being frustrated, and ask God for courage to express your anger in acceptable ways.

▶ Forgive those who frustrated you in the past and release your anger to God. Accept the sufficiency of His love to affirm your value.

If you feel a sense of frustration with life and long to feel accepted and significant, remember ...

▶ Proverbs 21:3—*"To do what is right and just is more acceptable to the Lord than sacrifice."*

▶ Galatians 1:10—*"Am I now trying to win the approval of men, or of God? Or am I trying to please men? If I were still trying to please men, I would not be a servant of Christ."*

▶ Psalm 25:9—*"He guides the humble in what is right and teaches them his way."*

▶ Lamentations 3:22–23—*"Because of the LORD's great love we are not consumed, for his compassions never fail. They are new every morning; great is your faithfulness."*

HOW TO Apply the Quick Answer to Anger

Members of a First Response Team know the importance of having a "quick answer." In the face of calamity, firefighters must provide a quick response but remain cool under pressure.

When you sense a surge of anger, it's vital that you learn to respond quickly. If not, your anger could blaze out of control.

The possibility of out-of-control anger remains ever present. A spark of irritation can be ignited *intentionally* by hurtful people or even *unintentionally* by those who love you. God wants you to seek His answer for anger quickly before it burns the bridges of your relationships because ...

"A gentle answer turns away wrath,
but a harsh word stirs up anger."
(Proverbs 15:1)

The Quick Answer to Anger

If I had to boil down all efforts to manage anger to the most basic steps, I believe I could reduce the solution to two points: one question and one action step.

Step 1. Ask – Can I change this situation?

Step 2. Action – If you can, change it.
If you can't, release it.

Let's go back to the first step: Can you change what angers you? Answer *yes* or *no*—that's it.

Now consider the second step: If you answered yes, you are angry about something you can change—so change it.

If the door squeaks, oil it.

If the faucet leaks, fix it.

If you answered no, you are angry about something you cannot change—so release it.

If your house burns down, release it (the fear).

If your loved one dies, release it (the hurt).

If your house does burn down, only as you emotionally release the pain of your loss can you rebuild your life and possibly your home. Being angry because of a burned house or the death of someone dear will not change the situation. It will only make matters worse.

How do you release your anger? First, list what angers you—every person, every situation. Then, go to God

in all humility, refusing to demand your rights, rejecting any thought of revenge, and surrendering the situation and yourself to the Lord—past, present, and future. Although you may feel completely powerless, in reality you have the power to release your pain and anger to Him.

> "Cast all your anxiety on him because he cares for you." (1 Peter 5:7)

THE "RELEASING YOUR ANGER" PRAYER

"Lord Jesus, thank You for loving me.
Thank You for caring about me.
Since You know everything,
You know the strong sense of
(hurt, injustice, fear, and/or frustration)
I have felt about (name or situation).
Thank You for understanding my anger.
Right now, I release all of my anger to You.
I trust You with my future and with me.
In Christ's name I pray. Amen."

HOW TO Alleviate Your Present Anger

Like a firefighter's hose spraying water on a fire, working through the following eight "A's" can do much to douse the potentially dangerous effects of anger in your life. Firefighters are always equipped with a variety of hoses, each designed to handle different sized fires, with one goal in mind—alleviating threatening flames.

▶ Handlines are small hoses 1.5 to 1.75 inches in diameter.

▶ Booster lines are larger, rubber-jacketed hoses stored on reels.

▶ LDH (large-diameter hose), measuring about 5 inches in diameter and useful for supplying water from hydrants to pumper trucks, is the largest hose used by firefighters.[31]

Because "*anger* is one letter short of *danger*" (this saying is more than a catchy phrase), these words reflect a painful truth. Too many times the tongue has not been tamed, conversations have escalated out of control, and people and relationships have been damaged, if not destroyed. Proverbs tells us …

> "As charcoal to embers and as wood to fire,
> so is a quarrelsome man for kindling strife."
> (Proverbs 26:21)

Acknowledge Your Anger.

▶ **Be willing** to admit you have anger.

▶ **Be aware** of when you feel angry.

▶ **Become aware** of how you suppress or repress your anger either because of fear or pride.

▶ **Be willing** to take responsibility for any inappropriate anger.

Realize, "*He who conceals his sins does not prosper, but whoever confesses and renounces them finds mercy.*" (Proverbs 28:13)

Ascertain Your Style.

▶ **How often do you feel angry?**
(Often? Sometimes? Seldom? Never?)

▶ **How do you know** when you are angry?

▶ **How do others know** when you are angry?

▶ **How do you release** your anger?

(Do you explode? Do you criticize? Do you joke or tease? Do you become sarcastic, defensive, or teary-eyed?)

As you seek to identify the way you express your anger, pray, *"Test me, O Lord, and try me, examine my heart and my mind."* (Psalm 26:2)

Assess the Source.

▶ **Hurt:** Is the source of your anger hurt feelings from the words or actions of others?

▶ **Injustice:** Is the source of your anger the unjust actions of someone toward you or another person?

▶ **Fear:** Is the source of your anger fear due to a recent or anticipated loss?

▶ **Frustration:** Is the source of your anger frustration over blocked plans, hopes, or dreams?

Commit to total honesty before God. *"I know, my God, that you test the heart and are pleased with integrity."* (1 Chronicles 29:17)

Appraise Your Thinking.

▶ **Are you expecting others to meet your standards?**

- "She should take better care of her children."
- "He ought to notice what I do for him."
- "He must be here before 7:00 p.m."
- "She'd better not call during dinner!"

▶ Are you guilty of distorted thinking?

- Exaggerating the situation
- Assuming the worst
- Labeling one action based on other actions
- Generalizing by saying, "you never" or "you always"

▶ Are you believing lies?

- "God is punishing me for my past."
- "I don't deserve to be loved or successful."
- "My future depends on my ability to keep this job."
- "God isn't really interested in whether I'm fulfilled or not."

▶ Are you blaming God or others?

- "This situation is someone else's fault, not mine."
- "He is responsible for this mess."
- "She let this happen."
- "God let me down."

Remember, *"A wicked man puts up a bold front, but an upright man gives thought to his ways."* (Proverbs 21:29)

ADMIT YOUR NEEDS.

▶ Do you use manipulative anger as a ploy in an attempt to feel loved?

▶ **Do you use explosive anger,** insisting on certain conditions in order to feel significant?

▶ **Do you use controlling anger** to demand your way in order to feel secure?

▶ **Do you know that only Christ can ultimately meet all of your inner needs** for love, significance, and security?

Rest assured, *"My God will meet all your needs according to his glorious riches in Christ Jesus."* (Philippians 4:19)

ABANDON YOUR DEMANDS.

Instead of demanding that others meet your inner needs for love, significance, and security, learn to look to the Lord to meet your needs.[32]

▶ **Look to the Lord** to meet your need for love.

"Lord, though I would like to feel more love from others, I know You love me unconditionally, and you will love me forever."

"I have loved you with an everlasting love; I have drawn you with loving-kindness." (Jeremiah 31:3)

▶ **Look to the Lord** to meet your need for significance.

"Lord, though I would like to feel more significant to those around me, I know I am significant in Your eyes."

"'I know the plans I have for you,' declares the LORD, 'plans to prosper you and not to harm you, plans to give you hope and a future.'" (Jeremiah 29:11)

▶ **Look to the Lord** to meet your need for security.

"Lord, though I wish I felt more secure in my relationships, I know I am secure in my relationship with You."

"The LORD is with me; I will not be afraid. What can man do to me?" (Psalm 118:6)

▶ **Look to the Lord** to meet all of your needs for life and godliness.

"Lord, though I wish others would be more responsive to my needs, I know You have promised to meet all of my needs."

"His divine power has given us everything we need for life and godliness through our knowledge of him who called us by his own glory and goodness." (2 Peter 1:3)

Constantly remind yourself, *"God is able to make all grace abound to you, so that in all things at all times, having all that you need, you will abound in every good work."* (2 Corinthians 9:8)

ADDRESS YOUR ANGER.

▶ **Determine whether your anger is really justified.**

- Has a wrong been committed?
- Has anyone suffered hurt or injury?
- Has an injustice occurred?

    Consider, *"This is what the LORD Almighty says: 'Give careful thought to your ways.'"* (Haggai 1:5)

▶ **Decide on the appropriate response.**

- How important is the issue?
- Would a good purpose be served if I mention it?
- Should I acknowledge my anger only to the Lord?

Remember, *"[There is] a time to be silent and a time to speak."* (Ecclesiastes 3:7)

▶ Depend on the Holy Spirit for guidance.

- Ask for counsel about your anger.
- Ask for insight about your anger.
- Ask for wisdom about your anger.

  Feel confident about the role of the Holy Spirit in your life. *"The Spirit of truth ... will guide you into all truth. ... and he will tell you what is yet to come."* (John 16:13)

▶ Develop constructive dialogue if you need to confront an offender.

- Don't speak rashly with a heart of unforgiveness.

  Do think carefully or "care fully" before you speak cautiously.

- Don't use "you" phrases such as: "How could you?" or "Why can't you?"

  Do use personal statements such as
  "I feel _____" or "I need _____"

- Don't bring up past grievances.

  Do stay focused on the present issue.

- Don't assume the other person is wrong.

  Do listen for feedback from another point of view.

- Don't expect instant understanding.

  Do be patient and keep responding with a gentle tone of voice.

  "Through patience a ruler can be persuaded, and a gentle tongue can break a bone." (Proverbs 25:15)

ALTER YOUR ATTITUDES.

Read Philippians 2:2–8.

▶ Have the goal to be like-minded with Christ.

"Make my joy complete by being like-minded, having the same love, being one in spirit and purpose." (v. 2)

▶ Do not think of yourself first.

"Do nothing out of selfish ambition or vain conceit" (v. 3)

▶ Give the other person preferential treatment.

"... but in humility consider others better than yourselves." (v. 3)

▶ Consider the interests of the other person.

"Each of you should look not only to your own interests, but also to the interests of others." (v. 4)

▶ Have the attitude of Jesus Christ.

"Your attitude should be the same as that of Christ Jesus ..." (v. 5)

▶ Do not emphasize your position or rights.

"Who, being in very nature God, did not consider equality with God something to be grasped ..." (v. 6)

▶ Look for ways to serve with a servant's heart.

"... but made himself nothing, taking the very nature of a servant, being made in human likeness." (v. 7)

▶ Speak and act with a humble spirit.

"And being found in appearance as a man, he humbled himself ..." (v. 8)

▶ Obey the Word of God, and submit your will to His will.

"... and became obedient ..." (v. 8)

▶ Be willing to die to your own desires.

"to death—even death on a cross!" (v. 8)

HOW TO Communicate Your Anger to Another

A fire extinguisher is an effective tool for putting out small fires, but proper procedures must be followed. Remembering the acronym PASS will ensure that you are operating the extinguisher appropriately with maximum firefighting results:

P—PULL the pin.

A—AIM the extinguisher nozzle at the base of the flames.

S—SQUEEZE the trigger while holding the extinguisher upright.

S—SWEEP the extinguisher from side to side, covering the area of the fire with the extinguishing spray.

Learning how to convey anger appropriately will better help you put out the fires of your inflammatory relationships.

Before communicating your anger toward someone, take time to evaluate whether addressing it is necessary and appropriate and whether you think it will prove beneficial. Some people simply do not know how to handle anger directed toward them. They become either hostile and defensive, or weak and placating. Neither response solves anything. In fact, the result can be as if someone has pumped oxygen into your anger, enflaming it all the more.

If you want merely to vent your feelings and to release some pent-up steam, then pour out your heart to God and maybe to another trusted person, but not to the person with whom you are angry. If you decide to arrange a meeting, you will need to do certain things in preparation.

> "Righteousness goes before him
> and prepares the way for his steps."
> (Psalm 85:13)

▶ **Choose to be proactive.**

- Examine your motivation.
- Be realistic in your expectations.
- Know what you want to accomplish.
- Assess the legitimacy of your request.
- Rehearse how you will approach the subject.
- Anticipate possible reactions from the other person.
- Think through how you might respond to those reactions.
- Decide whether you are willing to live with any negative repercussions.
- Talk with a wise and trusted person if you are uncertain what to do.

▶ **Choose a time and place to talk.**

- Select a time and place convenient for both of you in an atmosphere conducive for listening and sharing.
- Meet on "neutral turf" so that both of you are likely to feel equal in power and importance.
- Allot sufficient time to address the concerns both of you have.

- Commit the time to God and seek His wisdom and understanding.

▶ **Choose to communicate your desires for open and honest communication and resolution.**

- Express your pain and anger in a loving, non-accusatory way without criticizing the person's character utilizing the "Sandwich Technique."

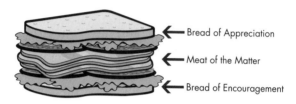

← Bread of Appreciation

← Meat of the Matter

← Bread of Encouragement

- Evaluate the willingness of the other person to receive your rebuke without becoming angry or defensive. Are they willing to understand your hurt, fear, frustration, or indignation over an injustice?

- Give opportunity for a response without interruption or defensiveness on your part.

- Affirm what is being said by repeating and clarifying spoken statements.

- Request any desired changes in behavior that you believe will resolve the present problem and prevent future problems.

- Agree to change any problematic behavior on your part.

- Promote fairness and objectivity, openness and optimism.

- Extend total forgiveness unreservedly and willingly.

- Value differences in goals, desires, and priorities.
- Applaud the person's willingness to listen to you, to resolve the problem, and to work toward improving your relationship.

Always keep in mind ...

"A word aptly spoken is like apples of gold in settings of silver." (Proverbs 25:11)

HOW TO Answer Common Questions about Anger

Ropes and ladders, axes and saws, are among the tools used by firefighters to rescue people, to free them from the bondage of burning buildings and the threat of being unable to escape. Firefighters are thoroughly trained in the area of rescue operations and through experience have come to know what tools are needed for what situation, all with the goal of helping others.

Likewise, turn your experiences with anger into a blessing, helping others understand they're not alone in their struggles, instilling hope that they, too, can be set free from raging anger. As you learn to face the fiery anger within and learn to act rather than react, God will not only use your anger to accomplish His purposes, but you will also be in a position to offer help and hope to others.

The questions below will help prepare you to give biblical answers to those who live in bondage to anger and who come to you for help and hope.

"Always be prepared to give an answer to everyone who asks you to give the reason for the hope that you have. But do this with gentleness and respect." (1 Peter 3:15)

Anger and Self-Control

QUESTION: **"What should I do when I feel my anger getting out of control?"**

ANSWER: Whenever you feel reason and self-control are giving way to irrational and unbridled behavior, put on the brakes and call a truce in order to take time out. Unless you do something to intervene in the process, the direction of the conversation will not change but will only escalate.

Stop and take a deep breath.

▶ **Hold up your hands** to indicate you are "surrendering" for the time being by calling a halt to what is taking place.

▶ **State slowly in a low tone** of voice (remember, "slow and low") that either you are getting too upset to think clearly or that the conversation is not going in a positive direction and does not seem to be resolving anything.

▶ **Explain** that you need to calm down and regain a cool head. Then take a walk around the block, retreat to a quiet place to listen to music, take a shower, or do whatever helps you regain your composure.

▶ **Agree on a time** to resume the conversation once you have regained your composure and have processed what has been said.

If you reach an impasse where agreement between the two of you is not possible ...

▶ **Agree** to have different opinions on the subject, but refuse to let those differences become a problem in the relationship.

- ▶ **Remember**, if two people agree on everything all the time, their relationship runs the high risk of becoming stagnant and void of growth.

- ▶ **Decide to engage** in stimulating conversations where varied opinions are expressed in order to develop listening skills, to learn from others, to think through your own opinions, and to practice expressing those opinions to others in a clear and concise (non-offensive) manner.

- ▶ **Commit** to valuing, accepting, and respecting each other as you grow in your understanding of one another.

> "A fool finds no pleasure in understanding but delights in airing his own opinions. ... Accept him whose faith is weak, without passing judgment on disputable matters."
> (Proverbs 18:2; Romans 14:1)

Anger and Road Rage

QUESTION: "How can I overcome road rage? I get so angry at other drivers!"

ANSWER: As drivers, we all have had someone cut in front of us, yell profanity at us, make obscene gestures toward us, or intentionally bump us. Whatever the situation, the moment you feel agitated, remove yourself from being in close proximity to the person and rehearse the truth in your mind.

- ▶ "I don't have to become angry. I know God will work this for my good as I keep my focus on Him."

- ▶ "I refuse to let someone else control my emotions. Lord, I surrender my emotions to Your control."

▶ "I choose to sing praises to God because He is in control, and I can remain calm and cool-headed."

▶ "Lord, I don't know what is wrong with this person, but I pray You will make Your presence known in this situation."

▶ "Lord, this person has a problem. I'm not going to let that problem become my problem. I choose instead to thank You for the gift of Your peace and provision."

▶ "I will stay calm in the strength of Christ. Thank You, Jesus, for Your Spirit within me, giving me everything I need."

"I can do everything through him who gives me strength." (Philippians 4:13)

Anger and Forgiveness

QUESTION: "I was severely wronged by someone I once trusted. People want me to forgive, but how can I ignore my anger and let this person off the hook?"

ANSWER: Picture a meat hook hanging around your neck and lying against your chest. Attached to the end of it is a burlap bag containing both your offender and all the pain this person has caused you. Do you really want to carry that person and all that pain with you for the rest of your life?

▶ The Lord wants you to take the anger and pain from the past and release it into His hands.

▶ Then He wants you to take the one who offended you off of your "emotional meat hook" and place

him onto God's hook. You can forgive him without trusting him. Forgiveness is given; trust is earned.

Extending forgiveness is based on your choice to be obedient to God and to release your anger to Him. Extending trust is based on another person's trustworthiness. Forgive everyone, but trust only the trustworthy. The Lord knows how to deal justly and effectively with all those who bring pain into your life. He says, *"It is mine to avenge; I will repay."* (Romans 12:19)

HOW TO Accept God's Aim for Anger

Forest rangers who care for and protect national parks occasionally say they have to "start a fire to stop a fire." Known as *backfires*, these fires help deprive the main fire of fuel and better enable forest rangers and firefighters to contain the blaze. At times God works for your good in much the same way. Ephesians 4:26 says, *"Be angry and do not sin."* (ESV)

God clearly intends for you to experience the emotion of anger and to use it for some positive purpose. For example, He can use your anger to spark your awareness of a blazing spiritual problem that needs to be snuffed out. God often allows fiery trials to test your faith and to develop the perseverance necessary to sustain your faith.

> "Consider it pure joy, my brothers,
> whenever you face trials of many kinds,
> because you know that the testing
> of your faith develops perseverance."
> (James 1:2–3)

FORGIVENESS PRAYER

*"Lord Jesus, thank You for caring about
how much my heart has been hurt.
You know the pain I have felt because of
(list every offense).
Right now I release all that
pain into Your hands.
Thank You, Jesus, for dying on the cross
for me and extending Your forgiveness to me.
As an act of my will, I choose to forgive (name).
Right now, I move (name)
off of my emotional hook onto Your hook.
I refuse all thoughts of revenge.
I trust that in Your time and in Your way
You will deal with my offender as You see fit.
And Lord, thank You for giving me
Your power to forgive so that I can be set free.
In Your holy name I pray. Amen."*

As you seek to allow God to direct your anger and use it for His purposes, remember ...

▶ **Anger** can bring your true feelings to light.

▶ **Anger** can uncover your need to set healthy boundaries.

▶ **Anger** can be used to bring positive change in your life.

▶ **Anger** can be the lens through which you gain insight into your past hurts.

▶ **Anger** can be the spark that encourages

healthy, appropriate, honest communication in relationships.

▶ **Anger** can be used by God to convict others of sin.

▶ **Anger** can reveal your inappropriate ways of trying to meet your own needs.

▶ **Anger** can be used by God to motivate others to make responsible decisions.

▶ **Anger** can be the foundation on which forgiveness is built.

▶ **Anger** can help you realize your need for the Lord.

As you allow God to use your anger for good, you will become an example to others and bring praise to God.

> "Let your light shine before men,
> that they may see your good deeds
> and praise your Father in heaven."
> (Matthew 5:16)

When you feel angry about an issue, if you can, change it—if you can't, release it. Release it into the hands of your sovereign Savior!

—June Hunt

What does **an angry, hot-tempered man** do?

> *"An **angry man** stirs up dissension, and a **hot-tempered** one commits many sins."* (Proverbs 29:22)

Why should I be **slow to become angry**?

> *"Everyone should be quick to listen, slow to speak and **slow to become angry**, for man's anger does not bring about the righteous life that God desires."* (James 1:19–20)

Regarding **anger**, what does **a fool** do in comparison to **a wise man**?

> *"**A fool** gives full vent to his **anger**, but **a wise man** keeps himself under control."* (Proverbs 29:11)

When could **anger give the devil a foothold** in my life?

> *"'In your **anger** do not sin': Do not let the sun go down while you are still angry, and do not **give the devil a foothold**."* (Ephesians 4:26–27)

Why should you not **be "quickly provoked in your spirit"**?

> *"Do not **be quickly provoked in your spirit**, for anger resides in the lap of fools."* (Ecclesiastes 7:9)

How does the Bible contrast **a hot-tempered man** and **a patient man**?

> "A **hot-tempered man** stirs up dissension, but a **patient man** calms a quarrel." (Proverbs 15:18)

Who shouldn't I **associate** or **make friends** with?

> "Do not **make friends** with a hot-tempered man, do not **associate** with one easily angered." (Proverbs 22:24)

How does the Bible contrast **a gentle answer** and **a harsh word**?

> "**A gentle answer** turns away wrath, but **a harsh word** stirs up anger." (Proverbs 15:1)

Since one of the psalms says, **"In your anger, do not sin,"** what should I do?

> "**In your anger do not sin;** when you are on your beds, search your hearts and be silent." (Psalm 4:4)

Why shouldn't I **rescue a hot-tempered man**?

> "A **hot-tempered man** must pay the penalty; if you **rescue** him, you will have to do it again." (Proverbs 19:19)

NOTES

1. Ray Burwick, *The Menace Within: Hurt or Anger?* (Birmingham, AL: Ray Burwick, 1985), 18; Gary D. Chapman, *The Other Side of Love: Handling Anger in a Godly Way* (Chicago: Moody, 1999), 17–18.

2. W. E. Vine, et al., *Vine's Complete Expository Dictionary of Biblical Words*, electronic ed. (Nashville: Thomas Nelson, 1996), s.v. "Nose."

3. Ibid., s.v. "Anger, Angry."

4. David R. Mace, *Love & Anger in Marriage* (Grand Rapids: Zondervan, 1982), 42–45.

5. James Mahoney, *Dealing with Anger* (Dallas: Rapha, n.d.), audiocassette; H. Norman Wright, Anger (Waco, TX: Word, 1980), audiocassette.

6. Gary Jackson Oliver and H. Norman Wright, *When Anger Hits Home* (Chicago: Moody, 1992), 84.

7. Chapman, *The Other Side of Love*, 19–22.

8. Scholastic, "Career as a Volcanologist," an interview with Dr. Stanley Williams, http://www2.scholastic.com/browse/article.jsp?id=4877.

9. For the following section see Burwick, *The Menace Within*, 33–50.

10. Michael Milstein, "Scientists Continue to Learn From Mount St. Helens," *The Oregonian* (January, 29, 2009), http://www.oregonlive.com/environment/index.ssf/2009/01/scientists_continue_to_learn_f.html

11. J. Carey, ed., *Brain Facts: A Primer on the Brain and Nervous System*, 5th ed. (Washington, D.C.: Society for Neuroscience, 2006), 28–30, http://www.sfn.org/skins/main/pdf/brainfacts/brainfacts.pdf.

12. Les Carter, *Getting the Best of Your Anger* (Dallas: Rapha, n.d.), audiocassette; Wright, Anger.

13. Milstein, "Scientists Continue…"

14. Wright, *Anger*, audiocassette.

15. Wright, *Anger*, audiocassette.

16. Lawrence J. Crabb, Jr., *Understanding People: Deep Longings for Relationship*, Ministry Resources Library (Grand Rapids: Zondervan, 1987), 15–16; Robert S.

McGee, *The Search for Significance*, 2nd ed. (Houston, TX: Rapha, 1990), 27–30.

17. Oliver and Wright, *When Anger Hits Home*, 97.

18. Wright, *Anger*, audiocassette.

19. McGee, *The Search for Significance*, 27; Crabb, *Understanding People*, 15–16.

20. Wright, *Anger*, audiocassette.

21. McGee, *The Search for Significance*, 27; Crabb, *Understanding People*, 15–16.

22. Wright, *Anger*, audiocassette.

23. Tony Sperling, "Fighting a Landfill Fire," *WasteAge* (Skokie, IL: Penton Media), January 1, 2001.

24. Sperling, "Fighting a Landfill Fire."

25. Sperling, "Fighting a Landfill Fire."

26. Chapman, *The Other Side of Love*, 21; Russell Kelfer, *Tough Choices* (San Antonio, TX: Into His Likeness, 1991), 59–60, 65.

27. Ronald T. Potter-Efron, *Angry All the Time: An Emergency Guide to Anger Control*, 2nd ed. (Oakland, CA: New Harbinger, 1994), 17.

28. David Powlison, "Anger Part 2: Three Lies About Anger and the Transforming Truth," *The Journal of Biblical Counseling* 14, no. 2 (Winter 1996): 18–21.

29. Crabb, *Understanding People*, 15–16; McGee, *The Search for Significance*, 27–30.

30. John Nieder and Thomas M. Thompson, *Forgive & Love Again: Healing Wounded Relationships* (Eugene, OR: Harvest House, 1991), 173–185; Robert Jeffress, *When Forgiveness Doesn't Make Sense* (Colorado Springs, CO: WaterBrook Press, 2000), 107–123.

31. International Association of Fire Chiefs and National Fire Protection Association, *Fundamentals of Fire Fighter Skills* (Sudbury, MA: Jones and Bartlett, 2009), 466.

32. Crabb, *Understanding People*, 15–16; McGee, *The Search for Significance*, 27–30.